Ladybird  Readers

Peter Rabbit and the Angry Owl

Series Editor: Sorrel Pitts
Text adapted by Sorrel Pitts

LADYBIRD BOOKS

UK | USA | Canada | Ireland | Australia
India | New Zealand | South Africa

Ladybird Books is part of the Penguin Random House group of companies
whose addresses can be found at global.penguinrandomhouse.com.
www.penguin.co.uk   puffin.co.uk   www.ladybird.co.uk

First published 2017
003

Peter Rabbit TV series imagery and text © Frederick Warne & Co. Ltd
& Silvergate PPL Ltd, 2017
Layout and design © Frederick Warne & Co. Ltd, 2017
The *Peter Rabbit* TV series is based on the works of Beatrix Potter
Peter Rabbit™ & Beatrix Potter™ Frederick Warne & Co.
Frederick Warne & Co is the owner of all rights, copyrights and trademarks
in the Beatrix Potter character names and illustrations

The moral right of the author has been asserted.

Printed in China

A CIP catalogue record for this book is available from the British Library

ISBN: 978-0-241-28369-1

Ladybird Readers

Peter Rabbit and the Angry Owl

Based on the
Peter Rabbit™ TV series

Squirrel
Nutkin

Lily

Peter
Rabbit

Old
Brown

Mrs. Tiggy-Winkle

Jeremy Fisher

forest

berry stains

berry trees

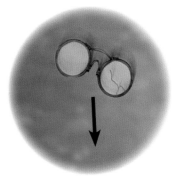

drop

5

Squirrel Nutkin was in the forest. Old Brown flew after him.

Old Brown tried to catch him.

"Help!" said Nutkin.

"Come into my house!" said Peter Rabbit. "Why does Old Brown want to catch you?"

"I took his glasses," said Nutkin, "and now I can't find them!"

"We can find them," said Lily.

"Thanks, my friends," said Nutkin.

"Let's go!" said Peter. The friends ran into the forest.

11

"Where did Squirrel Nutkin put the glasses?" said Peter.

"Let's ask Jeremy Fisher," said Lily.

"I'm sorry. I don't know," said Jeremy Fisher.

Then, Old Brown flew down from the sky.

"I want my glasses, Squirrel Nutkin!" he called.

"Come in here!" said Lily.

"Let's go!" said Peter, and all the friends ran behind him.

Old Brown flew after them, but he could not catch them.

"Come back here, Squirrel Nutkin!" he said.

"Where are Old Brown's glasses?" said Peter.

"Let's ask Mrs. Tiggy-Winkle," said Benjamin.

But Mrs. Tiggy-Winkle didn't know.

"Look!" she said. "Nutkin is putting berry stains on my clean clothes!"

Old Brown flew down from the sky again.

"There you are," he said.

He flew after Nutkin into the forest.

"Where are Old Brown's glasses?" said Peter.

"Nutkin made berry stains," said Lily. "Do you remember?"

"Yes!" said Benjamin. "We must go to the berry trees!"

The rabbits ran to the berry trees.

"Look! Here are the glasses!" said Peter.

Peter and his friends found Nutkin. Old Brown was with him.

"I want my glasses, Squirrel Nutkin!" said Old Brown.

"Come here, Old Brown!" said Peter. "I've got your glasses."

Then, Peter dropped
the glasses.

"No!" said Old Brown.

He flew down to his glasses.
Then, he flew into the trees.

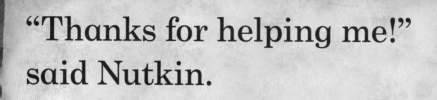

"Thanks for helping me!" said Nutkin.

"We're your friends!" said Peter. "We must always help you!"

Activities

The key below describes the skills practiced in each activity.

Spelling and writing

Reading

Speaking

? Critical thinking

Preparation for the Cambridge Young Learners Exams

1 Look and read. Put a ✓ or a ✗ in the boxes. 📖 ⭐

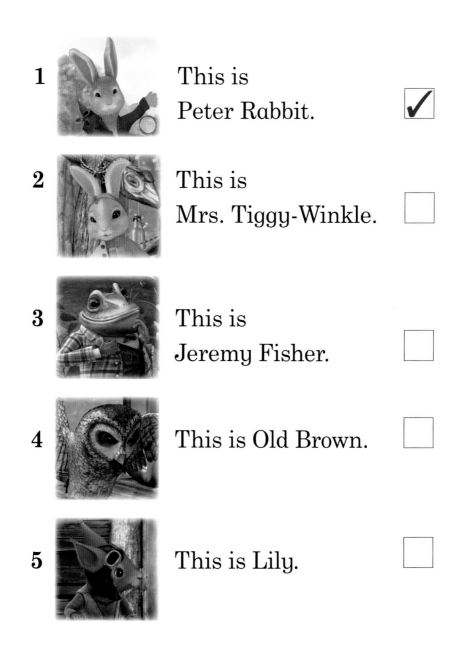

1 This is Peter Rabbit. ✓

2 This is Mrs. Tiggy-Winkle. ☐

3 This is Jeremy Fisher. ☐

4 This is Old Brown. ☐

5 This is Lily. ☐

Squirrel Nutkin was in the forest. Old Brown flew after him.

Old Brown tried to catch him.

"Help!" said Nutkin.

1 Squirrel Nutkin was in
the forest.   yes

2 Old Brown did not fly
after him.

3 Old Brown tried to
catch Nutkin.

4 "Help!" said Old Brown.

5 Old Brown can fly.

3 Match the sentences to the pictures. Write the missing words.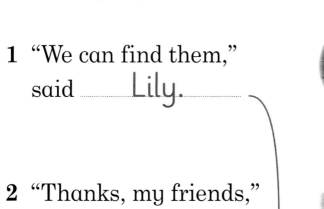

1 "We can find them," said ___Lily.___

2 "Thanks, my friends," said _____.

3 "Let's go!" said

_____.

4 The friends ran into the _____.

4 Choose the correct words and write them on the lines. 📖 ✏️ ✦

1 after	on	in
2 on	into	from
3 after	on	from
4 to	on	after
5 into	in	on

Old Brown flew ¹ __after__ Nutkin.

"Nutkin is putting berry stains
² _____ my clean clothes!"
said Mrs. Tiggy-Winkle.

Old Brown flew down ³ _____
the sky again.

"We must go ⁴ _____ the
berry trees!" said Benjamin.

Old Brown flew down to his glasses.
Then, he flew ⁵ _____ the trees.

5 Ask and answer the questions with a friend. 🗨

1

> *Who was in front of Lily?*

> *Peter was in front of Lily.*

2 Who was next to Squirrel Nutkin?

3 Who was in front of Squirrel Nutkin?

4 Where did the four friends go?

6 Find the words.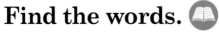

Old Brown
Lily
berry trees
forest
berry stains

litfjeOldBrownearberrystainsnberrytreesforesteLily

7 **Circle the correct words.**

1 **What** / **Who** did Old Brown say?

2 **Who** / **Where** said, "I want my glasses, Squirrel Nutkin!"?

3 **Who** / **Where** did Lily go?

4 **When** / **Who** was with the four friends?

5 **Who** / **Where** was Old Brown?

8 **Look at the letters. Write the words.** 📖 ✏️ ⬡

> y k s

1 Then, Old Brown flew down from the
   _____sky_____.

> e s g s l a s

2 "I want my _____!" he called.

> k i N u n t

3 Squirrel _____ did not have
   Old Brown's glasses.

> d i s a

4 "Come in here!" _____ Lily.

> F i e s r h

5 The three friends and Jeremy
   _____ went with Lily.

9 **Order the story. Write 1—5.**

_____ Old Brown flew after them.

1 "Let's go!" said Peter.

_____ Old Brown could not catch them.

_____ All the friends ran behind him.

_____ "Come back here, Squirrel Nutkin!" Old Brown said.

10 Talk about the two pictures with a friend. How are they different? Use the words in the box. ⬤

Old Brown   glasses   tree   chair
Lily and Benjamin   Squirrel Nutkin

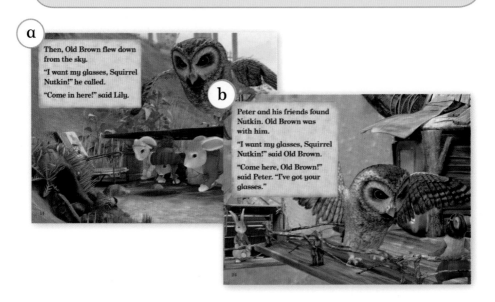

In picture a, Peter hasn't got Old Brown's glasses.

In picture b, Peter has got the glasses.

11 **Write the questions.**

are Where ? glasses Old Brown's

1 _Where are Old Brown's glasses?_

? Nutkin did Where them put

2 ....

down the sky flew from Who ?

3 ....

Peter ran Who ? behind

4 ....

flew ? the forest into Who

5 ....

12 Do the crossword.

Down

1 A place with lots of trees.

2 Squirrel Nutkin took these from Old Brown.

3 "We . . . find them," said Lily.

Across

1 Old Brown . . . down from the sky.

4 Nutkin put berry . . . on Mrs. Tiggy-Winkle's clean clothes.

13 **Choose the best answers.**

1 Peter and his friends found
  a Nutkin. **b** Benjamin. **c** Lily.

2 "I want my glasses, ...!"
  said Old Brown.
  a Peter
  b Squirrel Nutkin
  c Lily

3 "Come here, Old Brown!" said
  a Lily. **b** Nutkin. **c** Peter.

4 Then, Peter .... the glasses.
  a drop **b** dropped **c** drops

5 Old Brown flew into the
  a trees. **b** house. **c** sky.

14 **Match the two parts of the sentences.** 📖

1 "Why does Old Brown

α find them."

2 "We can

b always help you!"

3 "Where did Squirrel Nutkin

c on my clean clothes!"

4 "Nutkin is putting berry stains

d put the glasses?"

5 "We must

e want to catch you?"

15 **Look and read. Write _T_ (true) or _F_ (false).** 📖 ❂

1 Peter said, "Where are Old Brown's glasses?" ....T....

2 Benjamin made berry stains. ....

3 Lily said, "Nutkin made berry stains." ....

4 The rabbits ran to the berry trees. ....

5 Lily found the glasses. ....

16 **Read the questions. Write the answers.** 📖 ✏️

Lily   Peter Rabbit   Benjamin   Squirrel Nutkin

1 Who said, "We can find them."?

Lily said, "We can find them."

2 Who said, "Come into my house!"?

....

3 Who said, "Let's ask Mrs. Tiggy-Winkle."?

....

4 Who said, "Thanks for helping me!"?

....

17 **Talk about helping your friends.**

1 Do you like helping your friends?

Yes, I do.

2 Why did Peter say to Nutkin, "We must always help you!"?

3 Did a friend help you this week?

4 Did you say "Thank you."?

5 Did you help a friend this week?

47

Level 2

The Gingerbread Man	Sly Fox and Red Hen	The Monster Next Door	Wild Animals	Little Red Riding Hood
978-0-241-25442-4	978-0-241-25443-1	978-0-241-25444-8	978-0-241-25445-5	978-0-241-25446-2
Dinosaurs	Topsy and Tim The Big Race	Goes to the Treehouse	Sports Day	Going on a Picnic
978-0-241-25447-9	978-0-241-25448-6	978-0-241-25449-3	978-0-241-26222-1	978-0-241-26221-4
Peter Rabbit and the Angry Owl	Superhero Max	We Can Help!	Daddy Pig's New Van	School Trip
978-0-241-28369-1	978-0-241-28368-4	978-0-241-28367-7	978-0-241-28371-4	978-0-241-28372-1

Now you're ready for Level 3!